I0410936

Adaptive Harvest Management

Considerations for the 1998 Duck Hunting Season

PREFACE

The process of setting waterfowl hunting regulations is conducted annually in the United States. This process involves a number of meetings where the status of waterfowl is reviewed by the agencies responsible for setting hunting regulations. In addition, the U.S. Fish and Wildlife Service (USFWS) holds public hearings and publishes proposed regulations in the *Federal Register* to allow public comment. This document is part of a series of reports intended to support development of harvest regulations for the 1998 hunting season. Specifically, this report is intended to provide waterfowl managers and the public with information about the use of adaptive harvest management for setting duck-hunting regulations in the United States. This report provides the most current data, analyses, and decision-making protocols. However, adaptive management is a dynamic process, and information presented herein may differ from that published previously. Moreover, the set of regulatory alternatives has not yet been finalized for the 1998 hunting season and, therefore, harvest strategies presented in this report should be considered preliminary.

ACKNOWLEDGEMENTS

A working group comprised of technical representatives from the USFWS and the four Flyway Councils (Appendix A) was established in 1992 to review the scientific basis for managing waterfowl harvests. The working group subsequently proposed a framework of adaptive harvest management (AHM), which was first implemented in 1995. The USFWS expresses its gratitude to the working group and other individuals, organizations, and agencies that have contributed to the development and implementation of AHM. We especially thank D. J. Case and Associates for help with information and education efforts.

This report was prepared by the USFWS Adaptive Management & Assessment Team, which is administered by the Office of Migratory Bird Management and the North American Waterfowl and Wetlands Office. Fred A. Johnson was the principal author. J. P. Bladen, R. J. Blohm, D. F. Caithamer, D. J. Case, J. A. Dubovsky, K. Gamble, J. R. Kelley, W. L. Kendall, E. M. Martin, M. T. Moore, M. C. Otto, P. I. Padding, A. Romer, S. E. Sheaffer, G. W. Smith, and K. A. Wilkins provided information or otherwise assisted with report preparation. Comments regarding this document should be sent to Paul R. Schmidt, Chief, Office of Migratory Bird Management - USFWS, Arlington Square, Room 634, 4401 North Fairfax Drive, Arlington, VA 22203.

> **Cover art:** the 1935 duck stamp with a pen and ink drawing of canvasbacks
> by Frank W. Benson, who has been called the dean of American duck etchers.

TABLE OF CONTENTS

Annual reports on adaptive harvest management are available on the Internet at:
http://www.fws.gov/r9mbmo/reports/reports.html

EXECUTIVE SUMMARY

In 1995, the U.S. Fish and Wildlife Service (USFWS) embraced the concept of adaptive resource management for regulating duck harvests in the United States. The adaptive approach explicitly recognizes that the consequences of hunting regulations cannot be predicted with certainty, and provides a framework for making objective decisions in the face of that uncertainty. Moreover, adaptive harvest management (AHM) relies on the iterative cycle of monitoring, assessment, and decision making to clarify relationships among hunting regulations, harvests, and waterfowl abundance.

To date, AHM has focused primarily on midcontinent mallards, but progress is being made on extending the process to account for mallards breeding eastward and westward of the midcontinent region. The ultimate goal is to develop Flyway-specific harvest strategies, which represent an average of optimal strategies for each mallard breeding population, weighted by the relative contribution of each population to the respective Flyways. Geographic boundaries used to define midcontinent and eastern mallards have been established, and mathematical models of population dynamics are available for predicting regulatory impacts. Investigations regarding the geographic bounds and population dynamics of western mallards are ongoing.

A critical need for successful implementation of AHM is a set of regulatory alternatives that remain fixed for an extended period. When AHM was first implemented in 1995, three regulatory alternatives characterized as liberal, moderate, and restrictive were defined based on recent regulatory experience. The 1995 regulatory alternatives also were considered for the 1996 hunting season. In 1997, the regulatory alternatives were modified in response to requests from the Flyway Councils. Changes included provisions for additional hunting opportunity under the moderate and liberal alternatives, as well as the addition of a very restrictive alternative. For the 1998 season, the USFWS wishes to maintain the same regulatory alternatives as those considered in 1997, although a final decision is pending.

Preliminary harvest strategies were derived for midcontinent and eastern mallards, but they do not yet allow for Flyway-specific regulatory choices. The strategy for midcontinent mallards was based on: (1) an objective to maximize long-term harvest and achieve a population goal of 8.7 million; (2) an assumption that regulatory alternatives will remain the same as in 1997; and (3) current understanding of regulatory impacts. Based on a breeding population size of 10.6 million mallards and 2.5 million ponds in Prairie Canada, the optimal regulatory choice for midcontinent mallards in 1998 is the liberal alternative. The strategy for eastern mallards was based on: (1) an objective to maximize long-term harvest; (2) the regulatory alternatives for 1997; and (3) a "working model" of population dynamics. Based on a breeding population size of 1.0 million mallards and spring precipitation of 11.6 inches, the optimal regulatory choice for eastern mallards in 1998 also is the liberal alternative.

Future challenges include: (1) stabilization of regulatory alternatives for an extended period; (2) development of large-scale habitat monitoring programs; (3) further refinement of mallard population models; and (4) agreement on the appropriate scales of adaptive harvest management.

BACKGROUND

The annual process of setting duck-hunting regulations in the United States is based on a system of resource monitoring, data analyses, and rule making (Blohm 1989). Each year, monitoring activities such as aerial surveys and hunter questionnaires provide information on harvest levels, population size, and habitat conditions. This monitoring program represents the most comprehensive of its kind for any widely distributed group of wildlife species. Data collected from this monitoring program are analyzed each year, and proposals for duck-hunting regulations are developed by the Flyway Councils, States, and U.S. Fish and Wildlife Service (USFWS). After extensive public review, the USFWS announces a regulatory framework within which States can set their hunting seasons.

In 1995, the USFWS embraced the concept of adaptive resource management (Walters 1986) for regulating duck harvests in the United States. The adaptive approach explicitly recognizes that the consequences of hunting regulations cannot be predicted with certainty, and provides a framework for making objective decisions in the face of that uncertainty (Williams and Johnson 1995). Inherent in the adaptive approach is an awareness that management performance, in terms of sustainable hunting opportunities, can be maximized only if regulatory effects can be predicted reliably. Thus, adaptive management relies on the iterative cycle of monitoring, assessment, and decision making described above to clarify the relationships among hunting regulations, harvests, and waterfowl abundance.

In regulating waterfowl harvests, managers face four fundamental sources of uncertainty (Nichols et al. 1995a, Johnson et al. 1996, Williams et al. 1996):

(1) environmental variation - temporal and spatial variation in weather conditions and other key features of waterfowl habitat; an example is the annual change in the number of ponds in the Prairie Pothole Region, where water conditions influence duck reproductive success;

(2) partial controllability - the ability of managers to control harvest only within limits; the harvest resulting from a particular set of hunting regulations cannot be predicted with certainty because of variation in weather conditions, timing of migration, hunter effort, and other factors;

(3) structural uncertainty - an incomplete understanding of biological processes; a familiar example is the long-standing debate about whether harvest is additive to other sources of mortality or whether populations compensate for hunting losses through reduced natural mortality; structural uncertainty increases contentiousness in the decision-making process and decreases the extent to which managers can meet long-term conservation goals;

(4) partial observability - the ability to estimate key population variables (e.g., population size, reproductive rate, harvest) only within the precision afforded by existing monitoring programs.

Adaptive harvest management (AHM) was developed as a systematic process for dealing effectively with these uncertainties. The key components of AHM (Johnson et al. 1993, Williams and Johnson 1995) include:

4

(1)   a limited number of regulatory alternatives, which contain Flyway-specific season lengths, bag limits, and framework dates;

(2)   a set of population models describing various hypotheses about the effects of harvest and the environment on waterfowl abundance;

(3)   a measure of reliability (probability or "weight") for each population model; and

(4)   a mathematical description of the objective(s) of harvest management (i.e., an "objective function"), by which harvest strategies can be evaluated.

These components are used in an optimization procedure to derive a harvest strategy, which specifies the appropriate regulatory choice for each possible combination of breeding population size, environmental conditions, and model weights (Johnson et al. 1997). The setting of annual hunting regulations then involves an iterative process:

(1)   each year, an optimal regulatory alternative is identified based on resource and environmental conditions, and on current model weights;

(2)   after the regulatory decision is made, model-specific predictions for subsequent breeding population size are determined;

(3)   when monitoring data become available, model weights are increased to the extent that observations of population size agree with predictions, and decreased to the extent that they disagree; and

(4)   the new model weights are used to start another iteration of the process.

By iteratively updating model weights and optimizing regulatory choices, the process should eventually identify which model is most appropriate to describe the dynamics of the managed population. The process is optimal in the sense that it provides the regulatory choice each year necessary to maximize management performance. It is adaptive in the sense that the harvest strategy "evolves" to account for new knowledge generated by a comparison of predicted and observed population sizes.

MALLARD STOCKS AND FLYWAY MANAGEMENT

Since 1995, the AHM process has focused on midcontinent mallards, which are defined as those breeding in federal survey strata 1-18, 20-50, and 75-77, and in Minnesota, Wisconsin, and Michigan (Fig. 1). An optimal regulatory alternative for midcontinent mallards is based on breeding population size and prairie water conditions, and on the weights assigned to the alternative models of population dynamics. The same regulatory alternative is applied in all four Flyways, although season lengths and bag limits are Flyway-specific.

Efforts are underway to extend the AHM process to account for mallards breeding westward and eastward of the midcontinent survey area. These mallard stocks make significant contributions to the total mallard harvest, particularly in the Atlantic and Pacific Flyways (Munro and Kimball 1982). Extension of the current process to account for multiple mallard stocks and Flyway-specific regulatory choices involves:

(1)   augmentation of the decision criteria to include population and environmental variables relevant to eastern and western mallards;

(2)   revision of the objective function to account for harvest management objectives for mallards outside the midcontinent region; and

(3)   modification of the decision rules to allow independent regulatory choices in the Flyways.

An optimal harvest strategy for each Flyway then can be derived, which in effect would represent an average of the optimal strategies for each breeding stock, weighted by the relative contribution of each stock to the respective Flyways.

For the purposes of this report, eastern mallards are defined as those breeding in survey strata 51-54 and 56, and in New Hampshire, Vermont, Massachusetts, Connecticut, Rhode Island, New York, Pennsylvania, New Jersey, Delaware, Maryland, and Virginia (Fig. 1). Managers are in the process of establishing the geographic bounds of western mallards (see page 10).

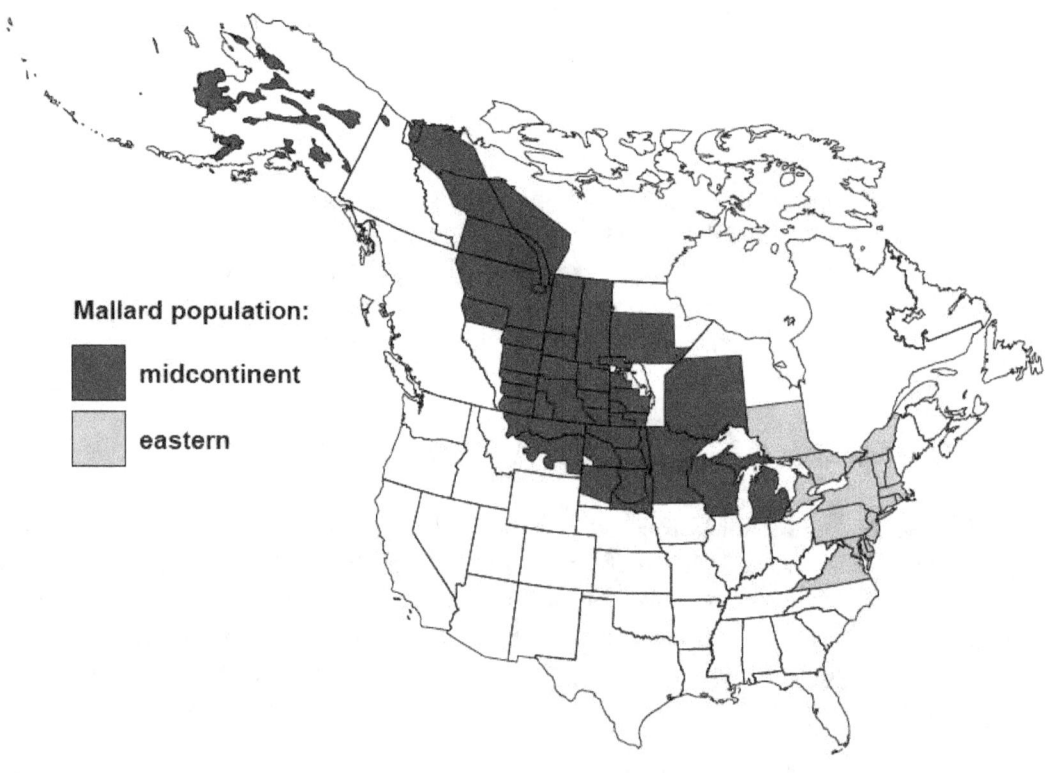

Fig. 1. Survey areas currently assigned to the midcontinent and eastern populations of mallards for purposes of harvest management.

MALLARD POPULATION DYNAMICS

Midcontinent Mallards

Estimates of the entire midcontinent population (as defined above) are available only since 1992. Since then, the number of midcontinent mallards has grown by an average of 8.9 percent (SE = 1.0) per annum (Table 1).

Table 1. Estimates[a] of midcontinent mallards breeding in the federal survey area (strata 1-18, 20-50, and 75-77) and the states of Minnesota, Wisconsin, and Michigan.

Year	Federal surveys		State surveys		Total	
	N	SE	N	SE	N	SE
1992	5976.1	241.0	977.9	118.7	6954.0	268.6
1993	5708.3	208.9	863.5	100.5	6571.8	231.8
1994	6980.1	282.8	1103.0	138.8	8083.1	315.0
1995	8269.4	287.5	1052.2	130.6	9321.6	304.5
1996	7941.3	262.9	945.7	81.0	8887.0	275.1
1997	9939.7	308.5	1026.1	91.2	10965.8	321.7
1998	9640.4	301.6	979.6	88.4	10620.0	314.3

[a] In thousands.

ly, the dynamics of midcontinent mallards are described by four alternative models, whic result fr   s
e   nt) about whether harvest is an additive or compensatory form of
m   nd whether the reproductive process is weakly or strongly density
d   lability limits reproductive success). The model with
ad   hunting mortality and weakly density-dependent recruitment ($S_A R_W$ t
conservative harvest strategy, whereas the model with compensatory hunting mortality and strongly density-dependent recruitment leads to the most liberal strategy ($S_C R_S$). The other two models ($S_A R_S$ and $S_C R_W$) lead to strategies that are intermediate between these extremes.

Two other sources of uncertainty in mallard harvest management are acknowledged. Unpredictability in environmental conditions is characterized by random variation in annual precipitation, which affects the number of ponds available during May in Canada. There is also an accounting for partial controllability, in which the link between regulations and harvest rates is imperfect due to uncontrollable factors (e.g., weather, access to hunting areas) that affect mallard harvest. A detailed description of the population dynamics of midcontinent mallards and associated sources of uncertainty are provided by Johnson et al. (1997).

A key component of the AHM process for midcontinent mallards is the updating of model weights.

These weights describe the relative ability of the alternative models to mimic changes in population size, and they ultimately influence the nature of the optimal harvest strategy. Model weights are based on a comparison of predicted and observed population sizes, with the updating leading to higher weights for models that prove to be good predictors (i.e., models with relatively small differences between predicted and observed population sizes) (Fig. 2). These comparisons must account for sampling error (i.e., partial observability) in population size and pond counts, as well as for partial controllability of harvest rates.

When the AHM process was initiated in 1995, the four alternative models of population dynamics were considered equally likely, reflecting a high degree of uncertainty about harvest and environmental impacts on mallard abundance. Model weights changed markedly in 1996, and have remained relatively stable since (Table 2). On the whole, comparisons of observed and predicted population sizes provide some evidence of strongly density-dependent reproduction, but little indication of a compensatory response to hunting mortality.

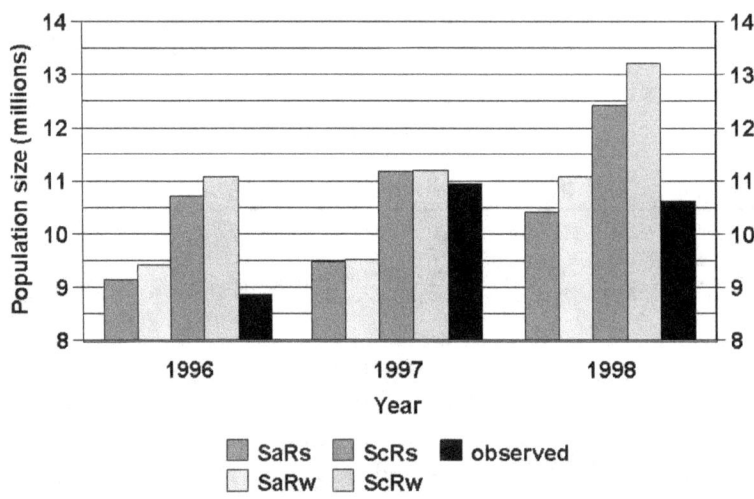

Fig. 2. Estimates of observed mallard population size (solid bar) compared with predictions from four alternative models of population dynamics (SaRs = additive mortality and strongly density-dependent reproduction; SaRw = additive mortality and weakly density-dependent reproduction; ScRs = compensatory mortality and strongly density-dependent reproduction; ScRw = compensatory mortality and weakly density-dependent reproduction).

Eastern Mallards

Midwinter counts and the Breeding Bird Survey provide evidence of exponential growth in the eastern mallard population since the mid-1970s. This pattern of growth also is apparent in the more recent fixed-wing (strata 51-54 and 56) and northeastern plot (New Hampshire south through Virginia) surveys (Table 3), although population growth seems to have slowed in more recent years.

Table 2. Temporal changes in probabilities ("weights") for alternative hypotheses of midcontinent mallard population dynamics.

Mortality hypothesis	Reproductive hypothesis	Model weights			
		1995	1996	1997	1998
Additive	Strong density dependence	0.2500	0.6417	0.5668	0.6462
Additive	Weak density dependence	0.2500	0.3576	0.4235	0.3537
Compensatory	Strong density dependence	0.2500	0.0005	0.0082	0.0001
Compensatory	Weak density dependence	0.2500	0.0002	0.0015	0.0000

Table 3. Estimates[a] of mallards breeding in the northeastern U.S. (plot survey from New Hampshire to Virginia) and eastern Canada (fixed-wing survey strata 51-54 and 56).

Year	Plot survey		Fixed-wing survey		Total	
	N	SE	N	SE	N	SE
1990	665.1	78.3	190.7	47.2	855.8	91.4
1991	779.2	88.3	152.8	33.7	932.0	94.5
1992	562.2	47.9	320.3	53.0	882.5	71.5
1993	683.1	49.7	292.1	48.2	975.2	69.3
1994	853.1	62.7	219.5	28.2	1072.5	68.7
1995	862.8	70.2	184.4	40.0	1047.2	80.9
1996	848.4	61.1	283.1	55.7	1131.5	82.6
1997	795.1	49.6	212.1	39.6	1007.2	63.4
1998	775.1	49.7	263.8	67.2	1038.9	83.6

[a] In thousands.

The population dynamics of eastern mallards were studied extensively by Sheaffer and Malecki (1996), but managers have not yet established a set of alternative models that characterize key uncertainties about the mortality and reproductive processes. In the interim, a "working model" has been developed to help managers understand the potential biological impacts of the current AHM process on eastern mallards.

The working model of eastern mallards incorporates natural mortality rates that are similar to those of midcontinent mallards and an assumption of completely additive hunting mortality. Reproductive rates are predicted based on the size of the population and regional precipitation during March-May of the current year. The reproductive process is characterized as strongly density dependent, predicting the highest reproductive rates during years in which population size is relatively low and spring precipitation is high. Mathematical details of the working model for eastern mallards are provided in Appendix B.

Western Mallards

The analyses necessary to incorporate western mallards into the AHM process are ongoing. Initial work has focused on delineating population boundaries by examining the geographic distribution of recoveries from birds banded in various breeding areas. Mallards banded in the Pacific Flyway states, British Columbia, the Yukon Territories, and southern Alberta have similar band-recovery distributions, suggesting they share breeding, migration, and wintering areas. This analysis has prompted concern over whether mallards in southern Alberta should be reassigned from the midcontinent to the western population. Recent analyses of banding and harvest data suggest that survival and productivity of breeding mallards in southern Alberta are similar to those in southern Saskatchewan, implying that southern Alberta is correctly aligned with the midcontinent population. In the next phase of investigation, efforts will be made to estimate reproductive and survival rates of mallards breeding in the Pacific Flyway states (including Alaska), the Yukon Territories, and British Columbia, and to identify important environmental factors influencing those rates.

HARVEST MANAGEMENT OBJECTIVES

Midcontinent Mallards

The basic harvest management objective for midcontinent mallards is to maximize cumulative harvest over the long term, which inherently requires conservation of population size. Moreover, the objective devalues harvest decisions that could be expected to result in a subsequent population size below the goal of the North American Waterfowl Management Plan (NAWMP) (Fig. 3). The value of harvest opportunity decreases proportionally as the difference between the goal and expected population size increases. This balance of harvest and population objectives results in a harvest strategy that is more conservative than that for maximizing long-term harvest, but more liberal than a strategy to attain the NAWMP goal regardless of losses in hunting opportunity. The current objective uses a population goal of 8.7 million mallards, which is based on the NAWMP goal of 8.1 million for the federal survey area and a goal 0.6 million for the combined states of Minnesota, Wisconsin, and Michigan.

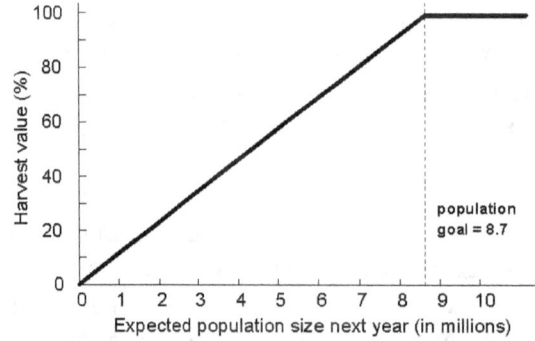

Fig. 3. The relative value of mallard harvest, expressed as a function of breeding-population size expected in the subsequent year.

Eastern Mallards

For the purposes of this report, the management objective for eastern mallards is to maximize long-term cumulative harvest. This objective is subject to change once the implications for average population size, variability in annual regulations, and other performance characteristics are better understood.

REGULATORY ALTERNATIVES

Evolution of Alternatives

When AHM was first implemented in 1995, three regulatory alternatives characterized as liberal, moderate, and restrictive were defined based on regulations used during 1979-84, 1985-87, and 1988-93, respectively (Appendix C, Table C-1). These regulatory alternatives also were considered for the 1996 hunting season. In 1997, the regulatory alternatives were modified to include: (1) the addition of a very restrictive alternative; (2) additional days and a higher duck bag-limit in the moderate and liberal alternatives; and (3) an increase in the bag limit of hen mallards in the moderate and liberal alternatives. For the 1998 season, the USFWS wishes to maintain the same regulatory alternatives as those used in 1997 (Table 4), although a final decision is pending (*Federal Register* 63:38705).

Mallard Harvest Rates

The most recent empirical estimates of mallard harvest rates are based on band-recovery data from 1979-93. Since 1995, harvest rates associated with the AHM regulatory alternatives have been predicted using these estimates, which have been adjusted to reflect differences in season length and bag limit, and for contemporary trends in hunter numbers (Table 5). These adjustments are not based on band-recovery data, but rather on estimates of hunting effort and success from hunter surveys. The reliability of these adjustments rests on the assumption that the ratio of total *harvests* achieved under any two regulatory alternatives is equal to the ratio of *harvest rates* obtained under the same two alternatives. The resulting predictions of harvest rates have large sampling variances, and their accuracy is uncertain.

Harvest rates for each of the 1998 regulatory alternatives were predicted assuming no change in the regulatory alternatives from 1997. However, expected harvest rates have changed due to revised analytical procedures, which more reliably account for current framework dates, and for the fall and winter distribution of mallards. The harvest-rate predictions changed most noticeably for eastern mallards, primarily due to an increase in the estimated proportion of eastern mallards harvested in the Atlantic Flyway.

Adult female mallards tend to be less vulnerable to harvest than adult males, while young are more vulnerable (Table 6). Estimates of the relative vulnerability of adult females and young in the eastern mallard population tend to be higher and more variable than in the midcontinent population.

Table 4. Regulatory alternatives being considered for the 1998 duck-hunting season.

	Flyway			
Regulation	Atlantic[a]	Mississippi[b]	Central[c]	Pacific[d]
Shooting hours	one-half hour before sunrise to sunset for all Flyways			
Framework dates	Oct 1 - Jan 20	Saturday closest to October 1 and Sunday closest to January 20		
Season length (days)				
Very restrictive	20	20	25	38
Restrictive	30	30	39	60
Moderate	45	45	60	86
Liberal	60	60	74	107
Bag limit (total / mallard / female mallard)				
Very restrictive	3 / 3 / 1	3 / 2 / 1	3 / 3 / 1	4 / 3 / 1
Restrictive	3 / 3 / 1	3 / 2 / 1	3 / 3 / 1	4 / 3 / 1
Moderate	6 / 4 / 2	6 / 4 / 1	6 / 5 / 1	7 / 5 / 2
Liberal	6 / 4 / 2	6 / 4 / 2	6 / 5 / 2	7 / 7 / 2

[a] The states of Maine, Massachusetts, Connecticut, Pennsylvania, New Jersey, Maryland, Delaware, West Virginia, Virginia, and North Carolina are permitted to exclude Sundays, which are closed to hunting, from their total allotment of season days.
[b] In the states of Alabama, Arkansas, Kentucky, Louisiana, Mississippi, and Tennessee, the season length and framework closing date under the moderate and liberal alternatives have not been finalized.
[c] The High Plains Mallard Management Unit is allowed 8, 12, 23, and 23 extra days under the very restrictive, restrictive, moderate, and liberal alternatives, respectively.
[d] The Columbia Basin Mallard Management Unit is allowed seven extra days under the very restrictive, restrictive, and moderate alternatives.

Table 5. Expected harvest rates (SE) of adult male midcontinent and eastern mallards under different regulatory alternatives, based on contemporary trends in hunter numbers. The predictions for 1998 are preliminary.

Mallard Population	Alternative	Regulatory alternatives considered for:		
		1995 and 1996	1997	1998
Midcontinent	Very restrictive	N/A	0.060 (0.015)	0.067 (0.014)
	Restrictive	0.084 (0.022)	0.084 (0.022)	0.869 (0.020)
	Moderate	0.103 (0.027)	0.112 (0.029)	0.111 (0.026)
	Liberal	0.123 (0.032)	0.139 (0.036)	0.133 (0.032)
Eastern	Very restrictive	N/A	0.084 (0.012)	0.130 (0.022)
	Restrictive	0.112 (0.016)	0.118 (0.017)	0.148 (0.024)
	Moderate	0.149 (0.021)	0.166 (0.023)	0.178 (0.027)
	Liberal	0.151 (0.031)	0.200 (0.028)	0.197 (0.030)

Table 6. Mean harvest vulnerability (SE) of female and young mallards, relative to adult males, based on band-recovery data, 1979-95.

Mallard population	Age and sex		
	Adult females	Young females	Young males
Midcontinent	0.748 (0.108)	1.188 (0.138)	1.361 (0.144)
Eastern	0.985 (0.145)	1.320 (0.264)	1.449 (0.211)

OPTIMAL HARVEST STRATEGIES

Midcontinent Mallards

The preliminary 1998 AHM strategy for midcontinent mallards was based on: (1) an assumption that regulatory alternatives are unchanged from 1997; (2) model weights for 1998; and (3) the dual objectives to maximize long-term cumulative harvest and achieve a population goal of 8.7 million (Table 7). This strategy provides optimal regulatory choices for midcontinent mallards assuming that all four Flyways would use the prescribed regulation. Ultimately, regulatory choices will be Flyway-specific by accounting for the relative contribution of the three mallard breeding populations to each Flyway. Overall, the 1998 harvest strategy is slightly more liberal than that for 1997, reflecting more confidence in the strongly density-dependent reproductive hypothesis (Table 2). The optimal harvest strategies for the 1995-97 seasons are provided in Appendix C (Tables C-2 to C-4) so that the reader can see how the strategy for midcontinent mallards has "evolved" over time.

Table 7. Optimal regulatory choices[a] for midcontinent mallards during the 1998 hunting season. This strategy is based on the assumption that regulatory alternatives are unchanged from 1997, current model weights (Table 2), and on the dual objectives of maximizing long-term cumulative harvest and achieving a population goal of 8.7 million.

Mallards[c]	Ponds[b]									
	1.5	2.0	2.5	3.0	3.5	4.0	4.5	5.0	5.5	6.0
≤5.0										
5.5							VR	VR	VR	VR
6.0			VR	VR	VR	VR	VR	R	R	R
6.5	VR	VR	VR	VR	VR	R	R	M	M	L
7.0	VR	R	R	R	R	M	M	L	L	L
7.5	R	R	M	M	M	L	L	L	L	L
8.0	M	M	M	L	L	L	L	L	L	L
8.5	M	L	L	L	L	L	L	L	L	L
≥9.0	L	L	L	L	L	L	L	L	L	L

[a] VR = very restrictive, R = restrictive, M = moderate, and L = liberal.
[b] Estimated number of ponds in Prairie Canada in May, in millions.
[c] Estimated number of midcontinent mallards during May, in millions.

Blank cells in Table 7 (and in other strategies in this report) represent combinations of population size and environmental conditions that are insufficient to support an open season, given current regulatory alternatives. In the case of midcontinent mallards, the prescriptions for closed seasons largely are a result of the harvest management objective, which emphasizes population growth at the expense of hunting opportunity when mallard numbers are below the NAWMP goal. However, limited harvests at low population levels would not be expected to impact long-term population viability. Therefore, the decision to actually close the hunting season would depend on both biological and sociological considerations.

We simulated the use of the harvest strategy in Table 7 with the four population models and current weights to determine expected performance characteristics. Assuming that harvest management adhered to this strategy, the annual harvest and breeding population size would average 1.3 (SE = 0.5) million and 8.1 (SE = 0.8) million, respectively.

Based on a breeding population size of 10.6 million mallards and 2.5 million ponds in Prairie Canada (and assuming regulatory alternatives remain the same as in 1997), the optimal regulatory choice for midcontinent mallards in 1998 is the liberal alternative.

Eastern Mallards

The preliminary 1998 AHM strategy for eastern mallards was based on: (1) an assumption that regulatory alternatives are unchanged from 1997; (2) the working model of population dynamics; and (3) an objective to maximize long-term cumulative harvest (Table 8). The strategy is slightly more conservative than that used last year, reflecting the increases in predicted harvest rates. Currently, this strategy only provides optimal regulations for eastern mallards under the condition that all Flyways would use the prescribed regulation. Ultimately, regulatory choices will be Flyway-specific by accounting for the relative contribution of eastern and midcontinent mallards to each Flyway.

We simulated the use of this harvest strategy with the working model of population dynamics to determine expected performance characteristics. Assuming that harvest management adhered to this strategy, the annual harvest and breeding population size would average 354 (SE = 74) thousand and 999 (SE = 95) thousand, respectively.

Based on a breeding population size of 1.04 million mallards and spring precipitation of 11.6 inches (and assuming that regulatory alternatives remain the same as in 1997), the optimal regulatory choice for eastern mallards in 1998 is the liberal alternative.

FUTURE CHALLENGES

Fixed Regulatory Alternatives

A critical need for successful implementation of AHM is a set of regulatory alternatives that remain fixed for an extended period. Frequent changes to the alternatives erode managers' ability to learn

Table 8. Optimal regulatory choices[a] for eastern mallards during the 1998 hunting season. This strategy is based on the assumption that regulatory alternatives are unchanged from 1997, the working model of population dynamics, and on an objective to maximize long-term cumulative harvest.

Mallards[c]	Spring precipitation[b]									
	6	7	8	9	10	11	12	13	14	15
500							VR	VR	VR	VR
550					VR	VR	VR	VR	R	R
600			VR	VR	VR	VR	R	M	M	L
650	VR	VR	VR	VR	R	M	M	L	L	L
700	VR	VR	R	M	M	L	L	L	L	L
750	R	R	M	L	L	L	L	L	L	L
800	M	M	L	L	L	L	L	L	L	L
850	M	L	L	L	L	L	L	L	L	L
>900	L	L	L	L	L	L	L	L	L	L

[a] VR = very restrictive, R = restrictive, M = moderate, and L = liberal.
[b] March to May precipitation in the northeastern U.S., in inches.
[c] Estimated number of eastern mallards in the combined fixed-wing and northeastern plot surveys, in thousands.

how regulations affect harvest and population size, and ultimately impact the ability to achieve management objectives. Recognizing the need to stabilize the set of alternatives, the USFWS and Flyway Councils expended considerable effort over the last two years to address concerns with the original set of regulatory alternatives. Based on comments received to date, the regulatory alternatives first considered for the 1997 hunting season appear to address most of those concerns.

During the last year, however, the USFWS came under increasing pressure to extend framework dates (the outside dates within which States must set their hunting season) beyond those specified in the current regulatory alternatives (*Federal Register* 63:29519-29520). In the interest of resolving the issue, the USFWS encourages the Flyway Councils to discuss framework dates from a national perspective. The USFWS believes that the National Flyway Council is the appropriate venue for this dialogue because the issue inherently involves perceptions regarding the fair and equitable distribution of hunting opportunity.

Large-scale Monitoring and Assessment of Waterfowl Habitat

Key to effective decision making within the AHM framework is at least some understanding of the linkage between population abundance (and other demographic variables) and sport harvest, habitat conditions, and other environmental features. This understanding is constructed from biological monitoring and assessment programs, and is codified in mathematical models that help predict the consequences of management actions. The monitoring and assessment programs used to guide waterfowl management in North America are among the best such programs in the world. Population-monitoring activities in particular are extensive and well focused, providing annual estimates of breeding-population size, hunter activity and harvest, and reproductive and survival rates.

However, mechanisms to monitor environmental conditions, and the effects of landscape changes, are not well developed. Beyond an aerial survey of water conditions in the Prairie Pothole Region, there are no systematic, large-scale programs to monitor important breeding or wintering habitats for waterfowl.

The migratory nature of waterfowl will necessitate large-scale, coordinated approaches to environmental monitoring, which can provide needed information at a variety of spatial and temporal scales (Johnson et al. 1996). Large-scale monitoring programs are expensive, however, and managers will need to rely on cost-effective remote sensing and GIS technologies. There have been some recent successes in using low-level videography and satellite imagery to monitor spatial and temporal variability in duck (Cowardin et al. 1995) and goose (Strong and Trost 1994) breeding habitat. To date, however, the USFWS has been unable to mobilize the expertise needed to explore various air and space-borne imaging platforms, data-management systems, habitat-recognition protocols, and methods for integrating physiographic and biological information. Therefore, the USFWS recently asked the National Aeronautics and Space Administration, through its Earth Science Strategic Enterprise, to support the application of remote-sensing programs for monitoring migratory-bird habitat changes on large geographic scales. If support is forthcoming, the effort would be coordinated by the new USFWS Adaptive Management and Assessment Team, which is housed at Patuxent Wildlife Research Center in Maryland.

Modeling Reproduction and Survival of Midcontinent Mallards

Reproduction--Current models used to predict reproductive success of midcontinent mallards include as independent variables only the number of ponds and the size of the breeding population. Although relationships between the number of duck broods and certain land-use variables (e.g., acreage of crops) have been identified at small (i.e., stratum-level) scales, detection of similar relationships between mallard age ratios and land-use variables measured at large scales has been elusive (M. W. Miller, unpublished data). These results suggest that the large-scale spatial context of landscape features may be important for predicting reproductive success. A recently-discovered relationship between the mallard age ratio and the mean latitude of the breeding population also supports this conclusion. Although landscape features other than pond numbers clearly could be useful for predicting mallard reproductive success, additional work is needed to identify relevant landscape features, as well as their appropriate spatial scale.

Survival--The current model set for midcontinent mallards includes two extreme forms of the following model:

$$S_i = S_0 (1 - \beta K_i)$$

where S_i is annual survival, S_0 is annual survival in the absence of hunting, β is a compensation coefficient ($\beta = 0$ implies total compensation and $\beta = 1$ implies total additivity of hunting mortality), and K_i = annual kill rate (Burnham et al. 1984). This model is useful in that it can be used to frame the debate over compensatory mortality (i.e., the model set for AHM includes $\beta = 0$ and $\beta = 1$). The disadvantages are that: (1) the appropriate value for S_0 under the two extreme models is unclear; and (2) there is some evidence that β changes over time, making it less useful for predictive purposes.

Current work is focusing on a more mechanistic model of survival, in which compensation for harvest is allowed as a function of density-dependent mortality during the non-hunting season (Johnson et al. 1993). A complicating factor in these investigations is that band-reporting rate, which is required to convert band-recovery rates to kill rates, varies geographically (Nichols et al. 1995b). Recognition of this variation has increased the number of model parameters that must be estimated, while making band-recovery data more sparse. This situation, in turn, has caused difficulties in producing estimates via existing computer programs. When these problems are resolved, the focus of the investigation will turn to the identification of appropriately scaled environmental variables that influence annual survival.

Modeling Reproduction and Survival of Eastern Mallards

Reproduction.--Among eastern mallards, there is a strong negative relationship between fall age ratios and indices of breeding-population size, suggesting a high degree of density dependence in reproduction. The nature of this relationship is important because the presence of strong density-dependence in population growth can lead to very liberal harvest strategies. Therefore, further investigations are needed to help understand whether the observed relationship actually represents cause and effect. Also, questions remain about the influence of environmental conditions on reproduction. To date, no weather variables have explained much of the variation in fall age ratios, and it is unclear whether these results reflect an insensitivity to weather conditions or a failure to identify the appropriate weather variable(s).

Survival.--There is some evidence that female mallards in the eastern population are more vulnerable to harvest than their midcontinent counterparts. However, it has been difficult to understand the spatial and temporal patterns (if any) of harvest vulnerability because band-reporting rates for female mallards in eastern North America are unknown. Until estimates of band-reporting rate are available, managers perhaps should consider sex-specific harvest vulnerability as a key source of uncertainty in population models for eastern mallards.

Ecological Variation and the Question of Management Scale

All ecological systems exhibit variability on a broad range of temporal, spatial, and organizational (or taxonomic) scales as a function of how individuals respond to their environment. The scale at which individuals are aggregated for harvest-management purposes is an arbitrary decision, but one that can strongly influence both the benefits and costs of management. Harvest management systems defined at scales that account explicitly for large amounts of biological variation will produce relatively high benefits, but also are characterized by high monitoring and assessment costs.

Determining the optimal scale for harvest management depends critically on the availability of explicit performance criteria (i.e., management goals, objectives, and constraints, including how harvest should be allocated among users) and on descriptions of how biological attributes vary among different scales. The description of biological patterns, in turn, involves the use of data to explore variation as a function of scale and to elucidate underlying causal mechanisms. The history of waterfowl harvest management has been characterized by persistent efforts to account for increasingly more spatial and organizational variation in waterfowl biology, but serious questions remain about the cost-effectiveness of this approach. Based on both technical and social considerations, the AHM framework may not be extended much beyond the three mallard stocks now under consideration.

Passive Versus Active Adaptive Management

The current protocol for AHM is *passively* adaptive, in the sense that any new knowledge about the impacts of hunting regulations is an unplanned by-product of the process. The recognition that some regulatory choices are more informative than others has led managers to consider more *actively* adaptive strategies (Nichols et al. 1995*a*, Williams and Johnson 1995). Actively adaptive strategies explicitly recognize that a reduction in management uncertainty is crucial to long-term success. Thus, development of such strategies involves a tradeoff between short-term management performance and the long-term value of knowing which alternative model of system dynamics is most appropriate. Actively adaptive strategies are expected to perform better than passive strategies when the management objective is based on an extended time frame (as in natural resource management). Recent advances in theory and software have overcome some of the limitations in computing actively adaptive strategies, and the AHM working group has begun to explore differences between passive and active strategies for midcontinent mallards. In analyses to date, there appears to be a fairly broad range of abundance in both midcontinent mallards and Canadian ponds where there is little or no difference in passive and active policies. Under some conditions, however, the actively adaptive policy is either more liberal or more restrictive than the corresponding passive policy. For the 1998 hunting season, there is no difference in the optimal regulatory choice between a passively adaptive and an actively adaptive strategy. Further work is needed, however, to clarify the differences between passive and active policies as a function of model weights, management objectives, planning horizons, and other AHM features.

LITERATURE CITED

Blohm, R. J. 1989. Introduction to harvest - understanding surveys and season setting. Proc. Inter. Waterfowl Symp. 6:118-133.

Burnham, K. P., G. C. White, and D. R. Anderson. 1984. Estimating the effect of hunting on annual survival rates of adult mallards. J. Wildl. Manage. 48:350-361.

Cowardin, L. M., T. L. Shaffer, and P. M. Arnold. 1995. Evaluations of duck habitat and estimation of duck population sizes with a remote-sensing-based system. Natl. Bio. Ser. Sci. Rep. 2. 26pp.

Johnson, F.A., C. T. Moore, W. L. Kendall, J. A. Dubovsky, D. F. Caithamer, J. R. Kelley, Jr., and B. K. Williams. 1997. Uncertainty and the management of mallard harvests. J. Wildl. Manage. 61:202-216.

_____, B. K. Williams, J. D. Nichols, J. E. Hines, W. L. Kendall, G. W. Smith, and D. F. Caithamer. 1993. Developing an adaptive management strategy for harvesting waterfowl in North America. Trans. North Am. Wildl. Nat. Resour. Conf. 58:565-583.

_____, _____, and P. R. Schmidt. 1996. Adaptive decision-making in waterfowl harvest and habitat management. Proc. Inter. Waterfowl Symp. 7:26-33.

Munro, R. E., and C. F. Kimball. 1982. Population ecology of the mallard. VII. Distribution and derivation of the harvest. U.S. Fish and Wildl. Serv. Resour. Pub. 147. 127pp.

Nichols, J. D., F. A. Johnson, and B. K. Williams. 1995*a*. Managing North American waterfowl in the face of uncertainty. Ann. Rev. Ecol. Syst. 26:177-199.

_____, R. E. Reynolds, R. J. Blohm, R. E. Trost, J. E. Hines, and J. P. Bladen. 1995*b*. Geographic variation in band reporting rates for mallards based on reward banding. J. Wildl. Manage. 59:697-708.

Sheaffer, S. E., and R. A. Malecki. 1996. Quantitative models for adaptive harvest management of mallards in eastern North America. New York Coop. Fish and Wildl. Res. Unit, Cornell Univ., Ithaca, unpubl. rep. 116pp.

Strong, L.L., and R.E. Trost. 1994. Forecasting production of Arctic nesting geese by monitoring snow cover with Advanced Very High Resolution Radiometer data. Pages 425-430 *in* Proc. PECORA 12 Symposium, Land Information from Space-Based Systems, Amer. Soc. Photogrammetry, Bethesda, Md.

Walters, C. J. 1986. Adaptive management of renewable resources. MacMillan Publ. Co., New York, N.Y. 374pp.

Williams, B. K., and F. A. Johnson. 1995. Adaptive management and the regulation of waterfowl harvests. Wildl. Soc. Bull. 23:430-436.

_____, _____, and K. Wilkins. 1996. Uncertainty and the adaptive management of waterfowl harvests. J. Wildl. Manage. 60:223-232.

APPENDIX A: AHM Working Group

Bob Blohm
U.S. Fish and Wildlife Service
Arlington Square, Room 634
4401 North Fairfax DriveArlington, VA 22203

phone: 703-358-1966
fax: 703-358-2272
e-mail: robert_blohm@fws.gov

Brad Bortner
U.S. Fish and Wildlife Service
911 NE 11th Ave.
Portland, OR 97232-4181

phone: 503-231-6164
fax: 503-231-2364
e-mail: brad_bortner@fws.gov

Frank Bowers
U.S. Fish and Wildlife Service
1875 Century Blvd., Suite 345
Atlanta, GA 30345

phone: 404-679-7188
fax: 404-679-7285
e-mail: frank_bowers@fws.gov

Don Brazil
Dept. of Wildlife, Fisheries, & Parks
P.O. Box 451
Jackson, MS 39205

phone: 601-364-2211
fax: 601-364-2008
e-mail: janice@mdwfp.state.ms.us

Dave Caithamer
U.S. Fish & Wildlife Service
11500 American Holly Drive
Laurel, MD 20708-4016

phone: 301-497-5865
fax: 301-497-5871
e-mail: dave_caithamer@fws.gov

Dave Case
D.J. Case & Associates
607 Lincolnway West
Mishawaka, IN 46544

phone: 219-258-0100
fax: 219-258-0189
e-mail: djcase@csi.com

Dale Caswell
Canadian Wildlife Service
123 Main St. Suite 150
Winnepeg, Manitoba, CANADA R3C 4W2

phone: 204-983-5260
fax: 204-983-5248
e-mail: dale.caswell@ec.gc.ca

John Cornely
U.S. Fish and Wildlife Service
P.O. Box 25486, DFC
Denver, CO 80225

phone: 303-236-8676
fax: 303-236-8680
e-mail: john_cornely@fws.gov

Gary Costanzo
Dept. of Game and Inland Fisheries
5806 Mooretown Road
Williamsburg, VA 23188

phone: 757-253-4180
fax: 757-253-4182
e-mail: gcostanzo@dgif.state.va.us

Jim Dubovsky
U.S. Fish & Wildlife Service
11510 American Holly Drive
Laurel, MD 20708-4017

phone: 301-497-5870
fax: 301-497-5706
e-mail: james_dubovsky@fws.gov

Joe Gabig
Game & Parks Commission
P.O. Box 30370
Lincoln, NE 68503-1417

phone: 402-471-5437
fax: 402-471-5528
e-mail: jgabig@ngpsun.ngpc.state.ne.us

Ken Gamble
U.S. Fish and Wildlife Service
608 Cherry Street, Room 119
Columbia, MO 65201

phone: 573-876-1915
fax: 573-876-1917
e-mail: ken_gamble@fws.gov

George Haas
U.S. Fish and Wildlife Service
300 Westgate Center Drive
Hadley, MA 01035-9589

phone: 413-253-8576
fax: 413-253-8480
e-mail: george_haas@fws.gov

Jeff Haskins
U.S. Fish and Wildlife Service
P.O. Box 1306
Albuquerque, NM 87103

phone: 505-248-6827 ext 30
fax: 505-248-7885
e-mail: jeff_haskins@fws.gov

Jeff Herbert
Dept. of Fish, Wildlife and Parks
1420 East 6th Avenue
Helena, MT 59620

phone: 406-444-2612
fax: 406-444-4952
e-mail: jherbert@mt.gov

Dale Humburg
Dept. of Conservation
Fish & Wildlife Research Center
1110 South College Ave.
Columbia, MO 65201

phone: 573-882-9880 ext 3246
fax: 573-882-4567
e-mail: humbud@mail.conservation.state.mo.us

Fred Johnson
U.S. Fish & Wildlife Service
11510 American Holly Drive
Laurel, MD 20708-4017

phone: 301-497-5861
fax: 301-497-5706
e-mail: fred_a_johnson@fws.gov

Mike Johnson
Game and Fish Department
100 North Bismarck Expressway
Bismarck, ND 58501-5095

phone: 701-328-6319
fax: 701-328-6352
e-mail: mjohnson@state.nd.us

Jim Kelley
U.S. Fish & Wildlife Service
11500 American Holly Drive
Laurel, MD 20708-4016

phone: 301-497-5862
fax: 301-497-5871
e-mail: james_r_kelley@fws.gov

Bill Kendall
Patuxent Wildlife Research Center
11510 American Holly Drive
Laurel, MD 20708-4017

phone: 301-497-5868
fax: 301-497-5666
e-mail: william_kendall@nbs.gov

Bob Leedy
U.S. Fish and Wildlife Service
1011 East Tudor Road
Anchorage, AK 99503-6119

phone: 907-786-3446
fax: 907-786-3641
e-mail: robert_leedy@fws.gov

Mary Moore
U.S. Fish & Wildlife Service
206 Concord Drive
Watkinsville, GA 30677

phone: 706-769-2359
fax: 706-769-2359
e-mail: mary_moore@fws.gov

Jim Nichols
Patuxent Wildlife Research Center
11510 American Holly Drive
Laurel, MD 20708-4017

phone: 301-497-5660
fax: 301-497-5666
e-mail: jim_nichols@usgs.gov

Mark Otto
U.S. Fish & Wildlife Service
11500 American Holly Drive
Laurel, MD 20708-4016

phone: 301-497-5872
fax: 301-497-5871
e-mail: mark_otto@fws.gov

Paul Padding
U.S. Fish & Wildlife Service
10815 Loblolly Pine Drive
Laurel, MD 20708-4028

phone: 301-497-5980
fax: 301-497-5981
e-mail: paul_padding@fws.gov

Jerry Serie
U.S. Fish & Wildlife Service
12100 Beech Forest Road
Laurel, MD 20708-4038

phone: 301-497-5851
fax: 301-497-5885
e-mail: jerry_serie@fws.gov

Dave Sharp
U.S. Fish and Wildlife Service
P.O. Box 25486, DFC
Denver, CO 80225-0486

phone: 303-275-2385
fax: 303-275-2384
e-mail: dave_sharp@fws.gov

Sue Sheaffer
Coop. Fish & Wildl. Research Unit
Fernow Hall, Cornell University
Ithaca, NY 14853

phone: 607-255-2837
fax: 607-255-1895
e-mail: ses11@cornell.edu

Graham Smith
U.S. Fish & Wildlife Service
11500 American Holly Drive
Laurel, MD 20708-4016

phone: 301-497-5860
fax: 301-497-5871
e-mail: graham_smith@fws.gov

Bryan Swift
Dept.of Environmental Conservation
108 Game Farm Road, Building 9
Delmar, NY 12054-9767

phone: 518-439-8083
fax: 518-478-0142
e-mail: bryan.swift@dec.mailnet.state.ny.us

Bob Trost
U.S. Fish and Wildlife Service
911 NE 11th Ave.
Portland, OR 97232-4181

phone: 503-231-6162
fax: 503-231-6228
e-mail: robert_trost@fws.gov

Khristi Wilkins
U.S. Fish & Wildlife Service
11500 American Holly Drive
Laurel, MD 20708-4016

phone: 301-497-5557
fax: 301-497-5971
e-mail: khristi_a_wilkins@fws.gov

Dan Yparraguirre
Dept. of Fish & Game
1416 Ninth Street
Sacramento, CA 94244

phone: 916-653-8709
fax: 916-653-1019
e-mail: dyparrag@hq.dfg.ca.gov

APPENDIX B: Eastern Mallard Model

The working model for eastern mallards predicts population size (N) as measured in the combined federal and state waterfowl surveys in eastern Canada and the northeastern U.S. However, these surveys have not been operational long enough to permit estimation of the relationship between abundance and reproductive rate. Therefore, the model relies on a Breeding Bird Survey (BBS) index, and its empirical relationship to N, to predict annual reproduction:

$$A(t) = 1.164646 - 0.200989 * BBS(t) + 0.085330 * SPRPPT(t) ,$$

where

> t = year,
> A(t) = predicted fall age ratio of females (young/adult),
> BBS(t) = 0.000004656 * N(t), and
> SPRPPT(t) = total precipitation (in inches) during March-May in the northeastern states.

SPRPPT is described as an independent, normally distributed random variable with mean = 10.7 and standard deviation = 4.0.

The model assumes complete additivity of hunting mortality, and predicts changes in population size using:

$$N(t+1) = N(t) * f(t) ,$$

where

$$f(t) = ((1 - sex) * ssf * (SHAF(t) + A(t) * (SHYF(t) + SHYM(t))) + sex * ssm * SHAM(t)) * sw ,$$

and where

> sex = 0.55 = mean proportion of males in the breeding population,
> ssf = 0.71 = summer survival of females,
> ssm = 0.90 = summer survival of males,
> sw = 0.90 = winter survival,
> SHAF(t) = hunting-season survival of adult females,
> SHYF(t) = hunting-season survival of young females,
> SHYM(t) = hunting-season survival of young males, and
> SHAM(t) = hunting-season survival of adult males.

Hunting-season survival rates are calculated using harvest rates predicted for each regulatory alternative, which are adjusted to account for a crippling loss of 20 percent.

APPENDIX C: Past Regulations and Harvest Strategies

Table C-1. Regulatory alternatives considered for the 1995 and 1996 duck-hunting seasons.

Regulation	Flyway			
	Atlantic	Mississippi	Central[a]	Pacific[b]
Shooting hours	one-half hour before sunrise to sunset for all Flyways			
Framework dates	Oct 1 - Jan 20	Saturday closest to October 1 and Sunday closest to January 20		
Season length (days)				
Restrictive	30	30	39	59
Moderate	40	40	51	79
Liberal	50	50	60	93
Bag limit (total / mallard / female mallard)				
Restrictive	3 / 3 / 1	3 / 2 / 1	3 / 3 / 1	4 / 3 / 1
Moderate	4 / 4 / 1	4 / 3 / 1	4 / 4 / 1	5 / 4 / 1
Liberal	5 / 5 / 1	5 / 4 / 1	5 / 5 / 1	6-7[c] / 6-7[c] / 1

[a] The High Plains Mallard Management Unit was allowed 12, 16, and 23 extra days under the restrictive, moderate, and liberal alternatives, respectively.
[b] The Columbia Basin Mallard Management Unit was allowed seven extra days under all three alternatives.
[c] The limits were 6 in 1995 and 7 in 1996.

Table C-2. Optimal regulatory choices[a] for midcontinent mallards during the 1995 hunting season. This strategy is based on the regulatory alternatives for 1995, equal weights for four alternative models of population dynamics, and the dual objectives of maximizing long-term cumulative harvest and achieving a population goal of 8.7 million.

Mallards[c]	Ponds[b]									
	1.5	2.0	2.5	3.0	3.5	4.0	4.5	5.0	5.5	6.0
4.5	R	R	M	M	M	M	L	L	L	L
5.0	M	M	L	L	L	L	L	L	L	L
5.5	L	L	L	L	L	L	L	L	L	L
6.0	L	L	L	L	L	L	L	L	L	L
6.5	L	L	L	L	L	L	L	L	L	L
7.0	L	L	L	L	L	L	L	L	L	L
7.5	L	L	L	L	L	L	L	L	L	L
8.0	L	L	L	L	L	L	L	L	L	L
8.5	L	L	L	L	L	L	L	L	L	L
9.0	L	L	L	L	L	L	L	L	L	L
9.5	L	L	L	L	L	L	L	L	L	L
10.0	L	L	L	L	L	L	L	L	L	L
10.5	L	L	L	L	L	L	L	L	L	L
11.0	L	L	L	L	L	L	L	L	L	L

[a] R = restrictive, M = moderate, and L = liberal.
[b] Estimated number of ponds in Prairie Canada in May, in millions.
[c] Estimated number of midcontinent mallards during May, in millions.

Table C-3. Optimal regulatory choices[a] for midcontinent mallards during the 1996 hunting season. This strategy is based on the regulatory alternatives and model weights for 1996, and the dual objectives of maximizing long-term cumulative harvest and achieving a population goal of 8.7 million.

Mallards[c]	Ponds[b]									
	1.5	2.0	2.5	3.0	3.5	4.0	4.5	5.0	5.5	6.0
4.5										
5.0										
5.5							R	R	R	R
6.0				R	R	R	R	R	M	M
6.5	R	R	R	R	R	M	M	L	L	L
7.0	R	R	R	M	M	L	L	L	L	L
7.5	R	M	M	L	L	L	L	L	L	L
8.0	M	L	L	L	L	L	L	L	L	L
8.5	L	L	L	L	L	L	L	L	L	L
9.0	L	L	L	L	L	L	L	L	L	L
9.5	L	L	L	L	L	L	L	L	L	L
10.0	L	L	L	L	L	L	L	L	L	L
10.5	L	L	L	L	L	L	L	L	L	L
11.0	L	L	L	L	L	L	L	L	L	L

[a] R = restrictive, M = moderate, and L = liberal.
[b] Estimated number of ponds in Prairie Canada in May, in millions.
[c] Estimated number of midcontinent mallards during May, in millions.

Table C-4. Optimal regulatory choices[a] for midcontinent mallards during the 1997 hunting season. This strategy is based on regulatory alternatives and model weights for 1997, and on the dual objectives of maximizing long-term cumulative harvest and achieving a population goal of 8.7 million.

Mallards[c]	Ponds[b]									
	1.5	2.0	2.5	3.0	3.5	4.0	4.5	5.0	5.5	6.0
4.5										
5.0										
5.5									VR	VR	VR
6.0			VR	VR	VR	VR	VR	VR	R	R
6.5	VR	VR	VR	VR	VR	R	R	R	M	M
7.0	VR	VR	R	R	R	R	M	M	L	L
7.5	R	R	R	M	M	M	L	L	L	L
8.0	M	M	M	M	L	L	L	L	L	L
8.5	M	M	M	L	L	L	L	L	L	L
9.0	L	L	L	L	L	L	L	L	L	L
9.5	L	L	L	L	L	L	L	L	L	L
10.0	L	L	L	L	L	L	L	L	L	L
10.5	L	L	L	L	L	L	L	L	L	L
11.0	L	L	L	L	L	L	L	L	L	L

[a] VR = very restrictive, R = restrictive, M = moderate, and L = liberal.
[b] Estimated number of ponds in Prairie Canada in May, in millions.
[c] Estimated number of mid-continent mallards during May, in millions.

www.ingramcontent.com/pod-product-compliance
Lightning Source LLC
Chambersburg PA
CBHW080757290526
45790CB00008B/3480

www.ingramcontent.com/pod-product-compliance
Lightning Source LLC
Chambersburg PA
CBHW080732290526
45790CB00008B/3164